Colorful Flower Garden

Put flower stickers wherever you'd like in the garden.
Then, add butterfly and ladybug stickers.

Beach Day

Give the kids beach toy stickers. Then, add sea creature stickers on the beach.

example

Make a Pattern on the Cow

Put stickers on the cow to create a pattern.

Sticker

Good job!

Picture Puzzle

Puppy Play

Put each dog sticker on its matching shadow. Then, find toy stickers and give them to the dogs.

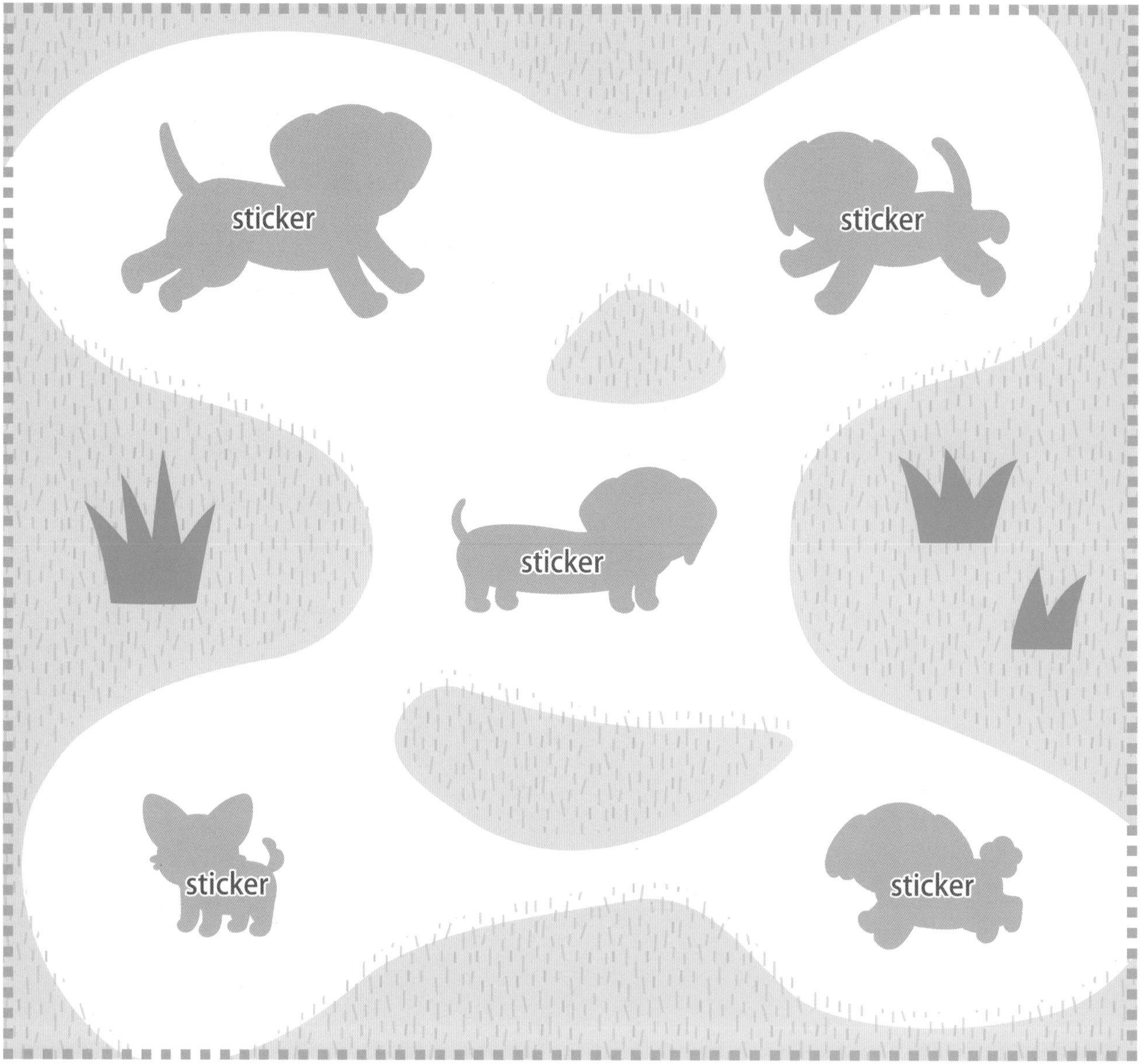

Picture Puzzle

Yummy Fruit

What fruit do you see? Put each fruit sticker on its matching shadow.

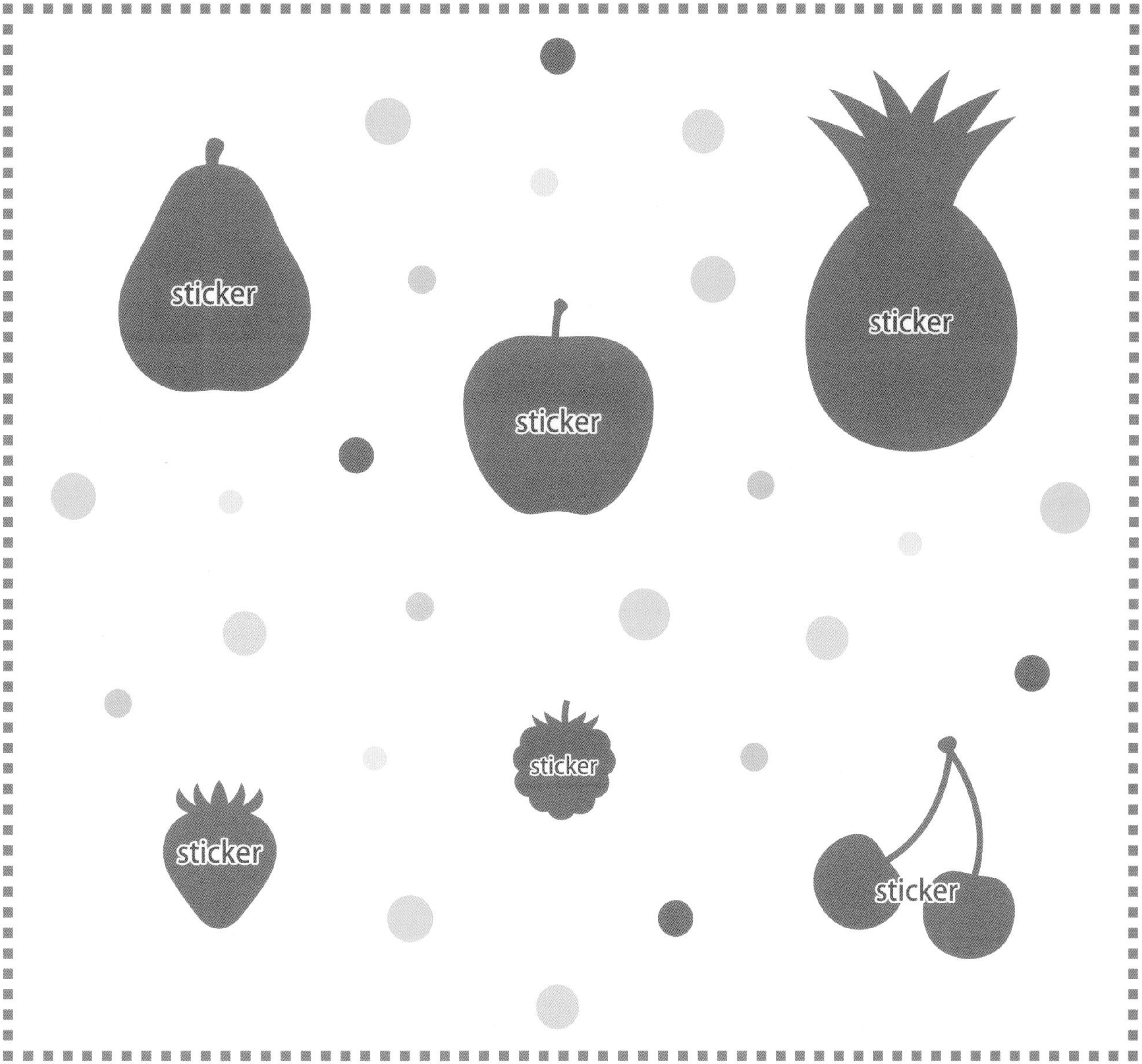

Matching Game

Match the Shadows

Find the stickers that match the shadows. Then, put one sticker in each box.

Sticker
Good job!

sticker | sticker

sticker | sticker

sticker | sticker

Animal Game

Put stickers on the pig and rabbit to complete the pictures.

Picture Puzzle

Picture Match

Add vegetable stickers to the bottom plate so it matches the top plate.

Picture Puzzle

Picture Match

Put animal stickers on the right so it matches the scene on the left.

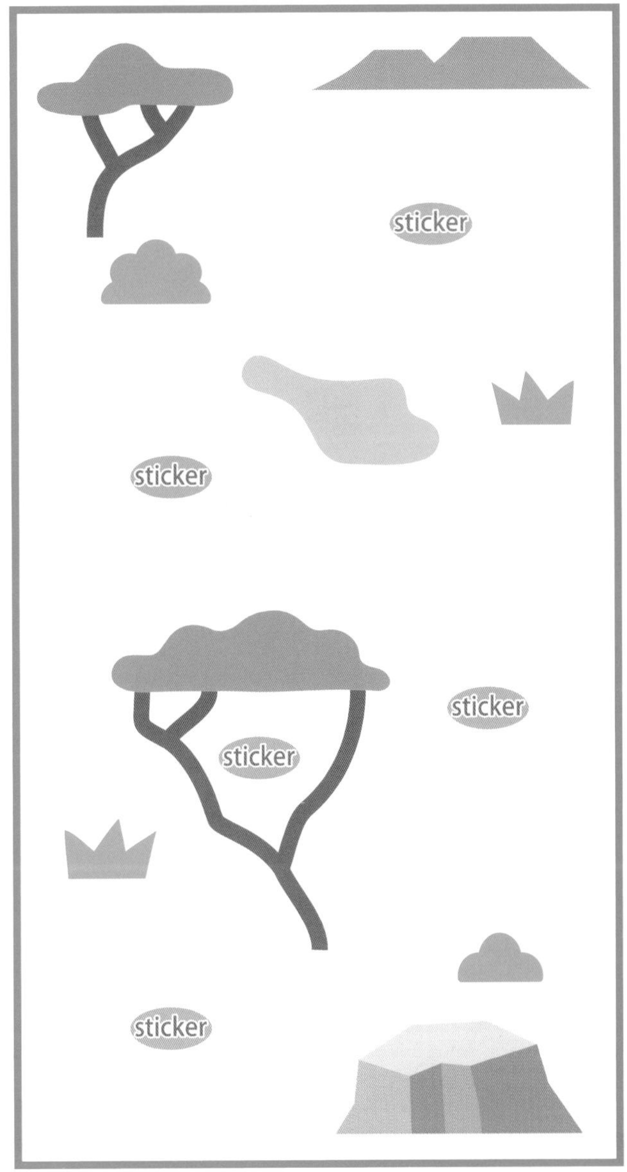

Matching Game

Animal Farm

Name the hiding animals. Then, put the matching animal sticker on the sticker next to it.

Matching Game

Sea Aquarium

Name the hiding sea creatures. Then, put the matching sea creature sticker on the sticker next to it.

Picture Puzzle

Complete the Picture

Put a sticker on sticker to complete each picture.

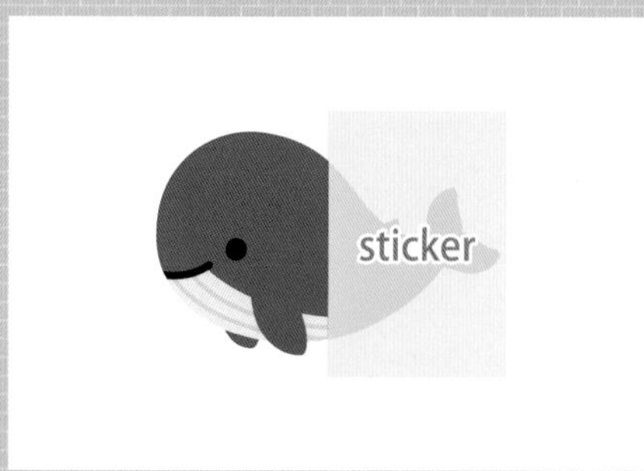

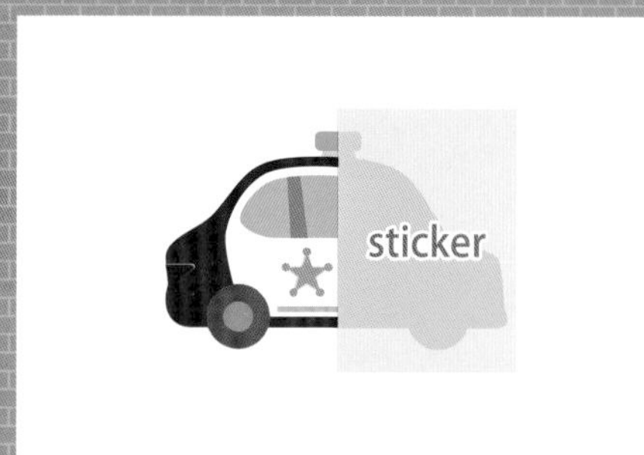

Creativity

Vegetable Friends

Add eyes, a mouth, and arms stickers to each vegetable.

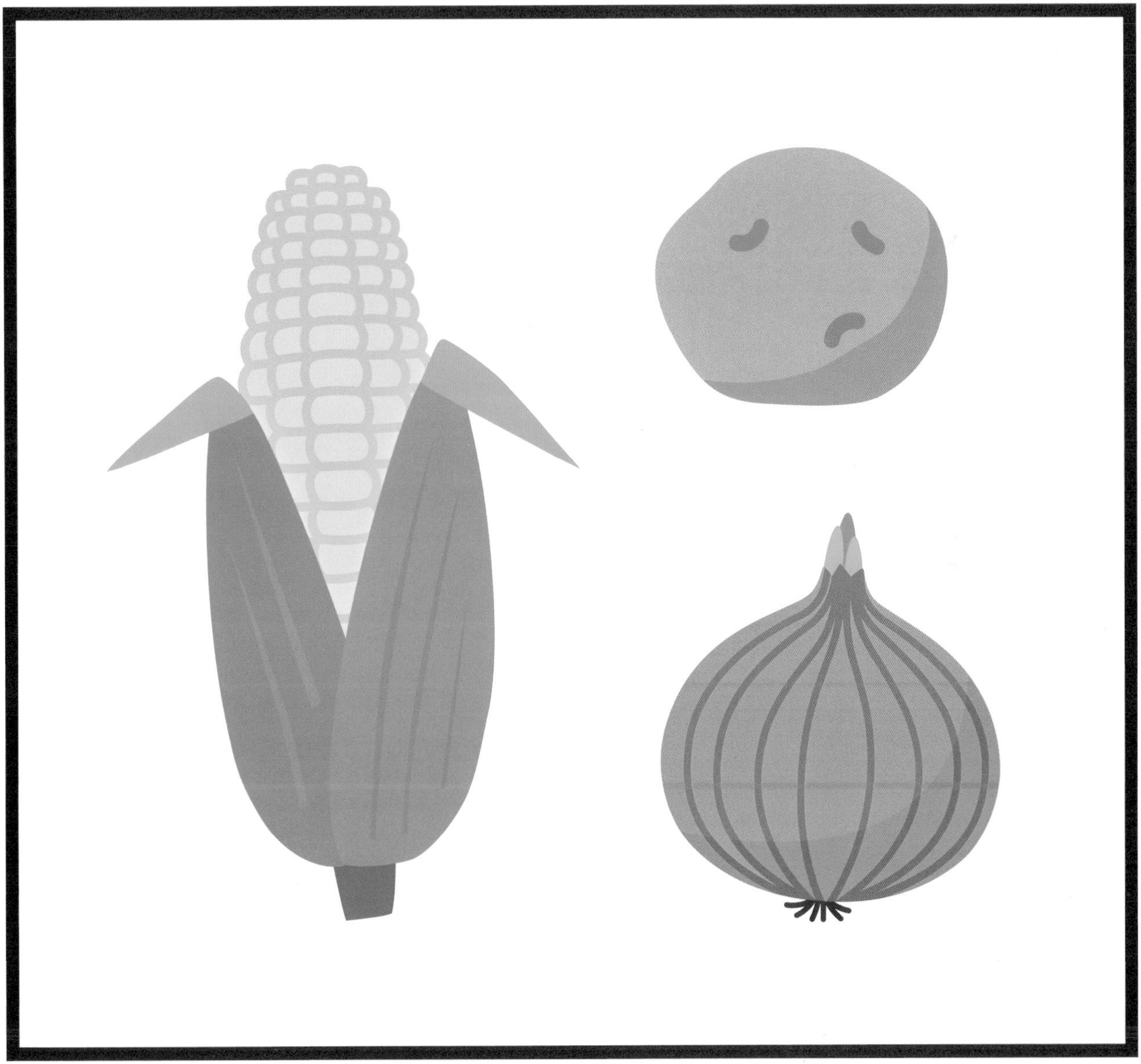

Numbers

Hungry Cats

Put a bowl sticker in front of each cat.

Numbers

Hats On

Put a hat sticker on each child.

Matching Game

Food Match

Put each sandwich sticker on the shape that matches its size. Then, put each hot dog sticker on the shape that matches its size.

Matching Game

Food Match

Put each apple pie sticker on the shape that matches it size. Then, put each cheeseburger sticker on the shape that matches its size.

Matching Game

Glove Pairs

Find the sticker that matches each glove to make a pair.

Matching Game

Shoe Pairs

Find the sticker that matches each shoe to make a pair.

Creativity

Make a Snowman

Complete the snowman by adding hat and scarf stickers. Then, add more snowball stickers to the snowy scene.

example

Creativity

Starry Sky

Put star stickers in the night sky. Then, add shooting star and moon stickers.

example

Letters

Things That Start with A

Say the name of each thing hiding behind the letter A. Then, put its matching sticker on the sticker .

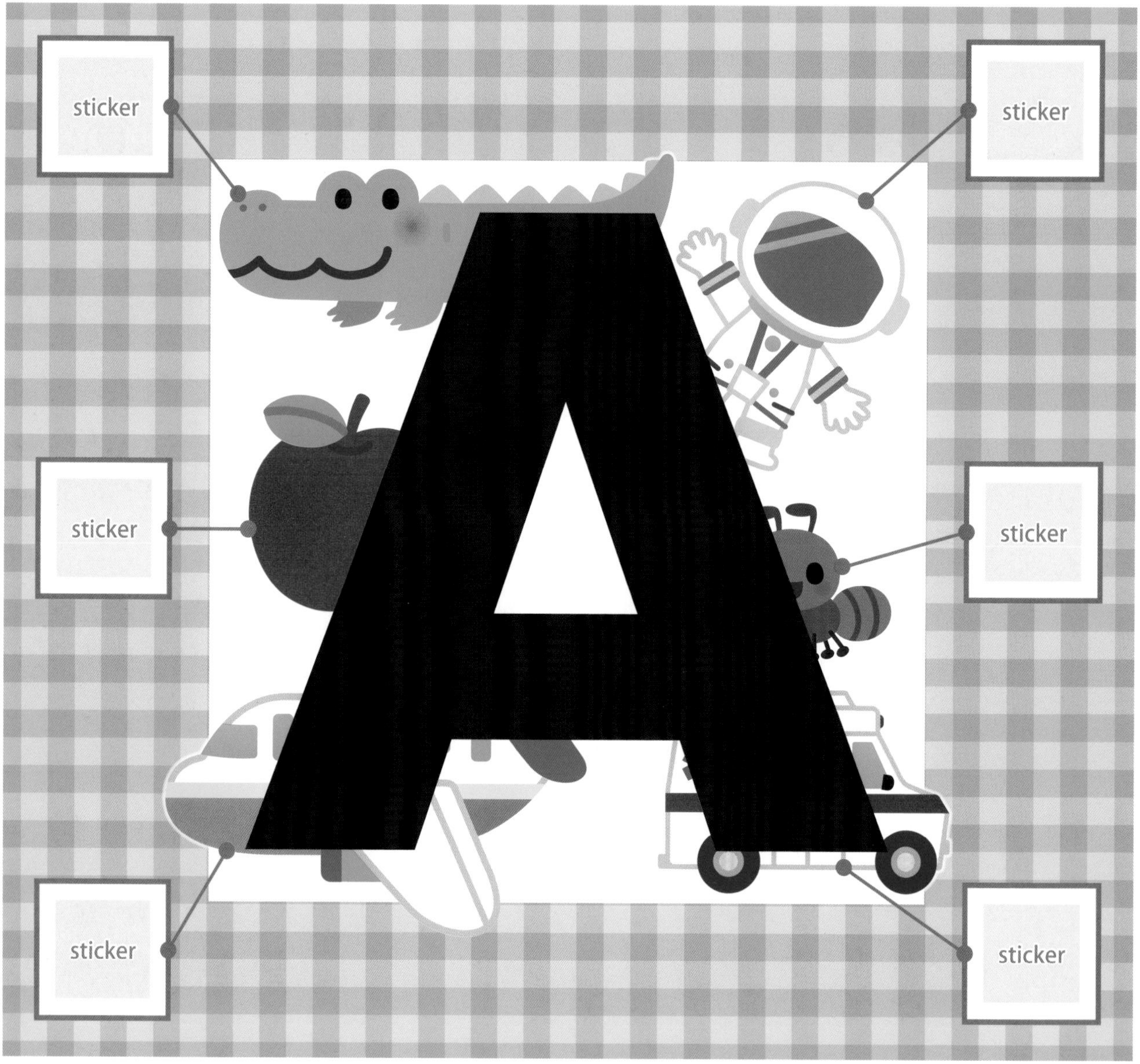

Letters

Things That Start with B

Say the name of each thing hiding behind the letter B. Then, put its matching sticker on the sticker .

Letters

ABC Maze

Follow the path in the order of the alphabet. As you go, put the letter stickers on the path. Then, put stickers on the matching sticker.

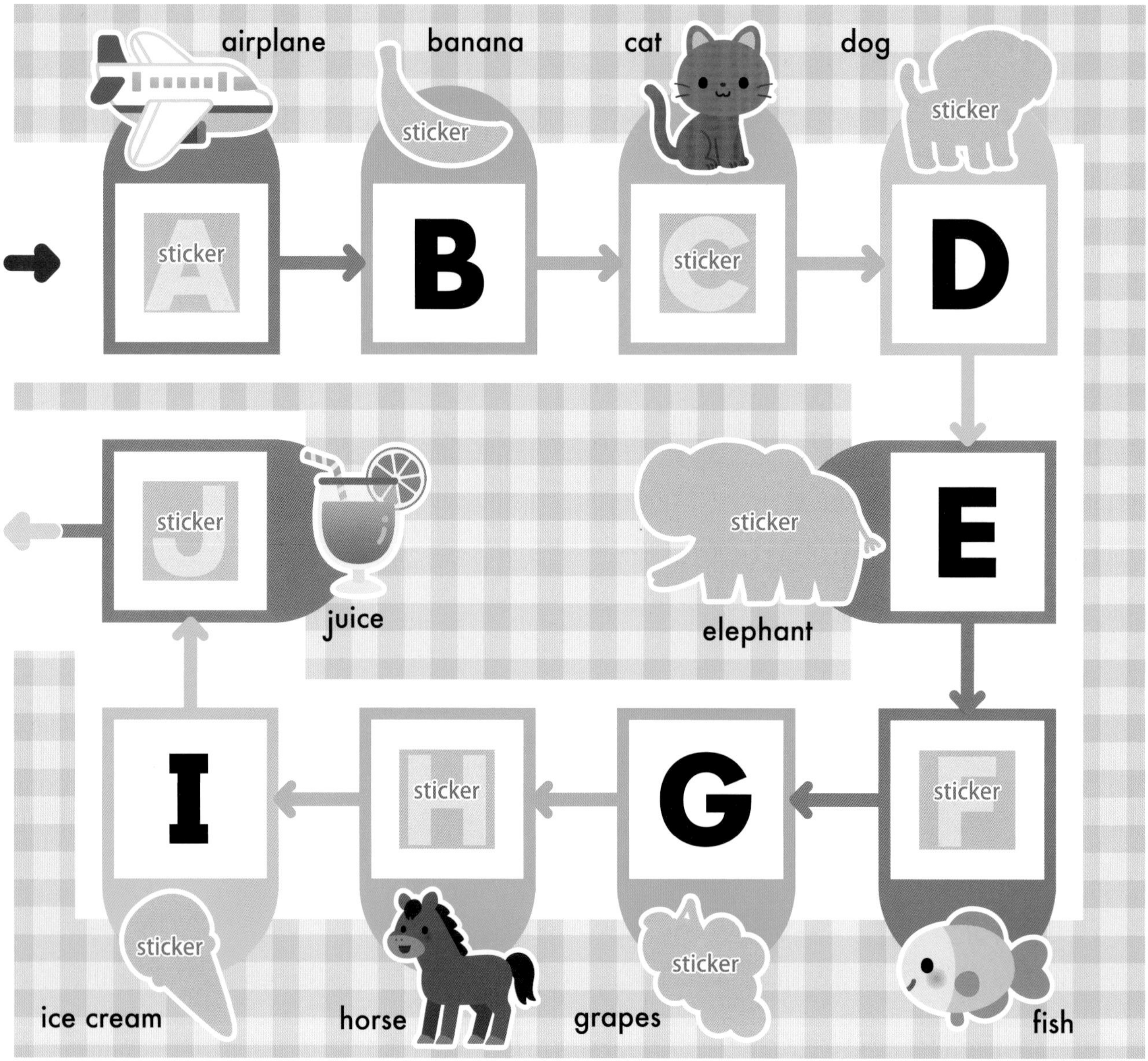

Numbers

Sweet Cookies

Add stickers so that each plate has 5 cookies.

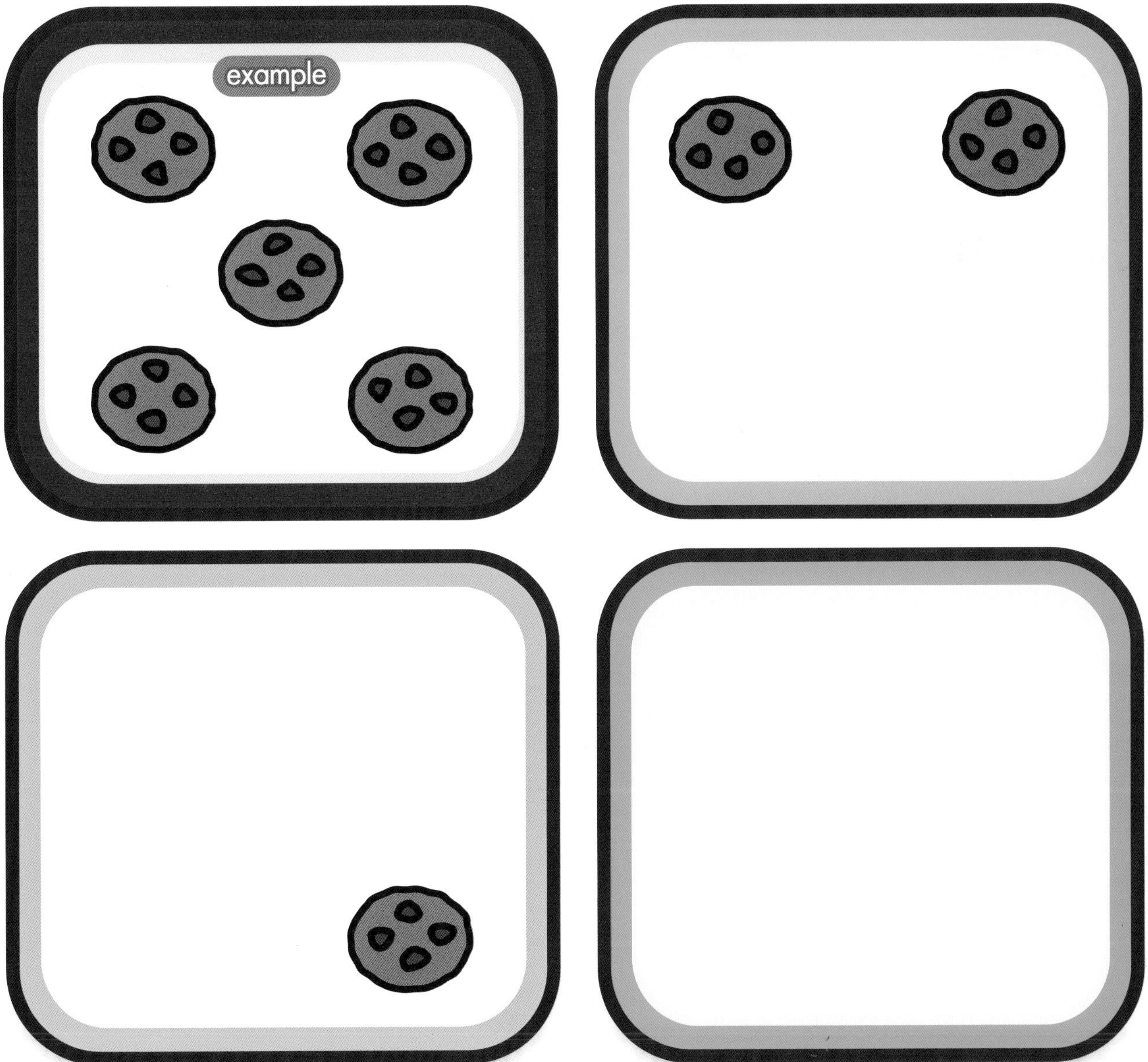

Numbers

Counting Flowers

Count the flowers. Add the number sticker to the box that matches the number of flowers.

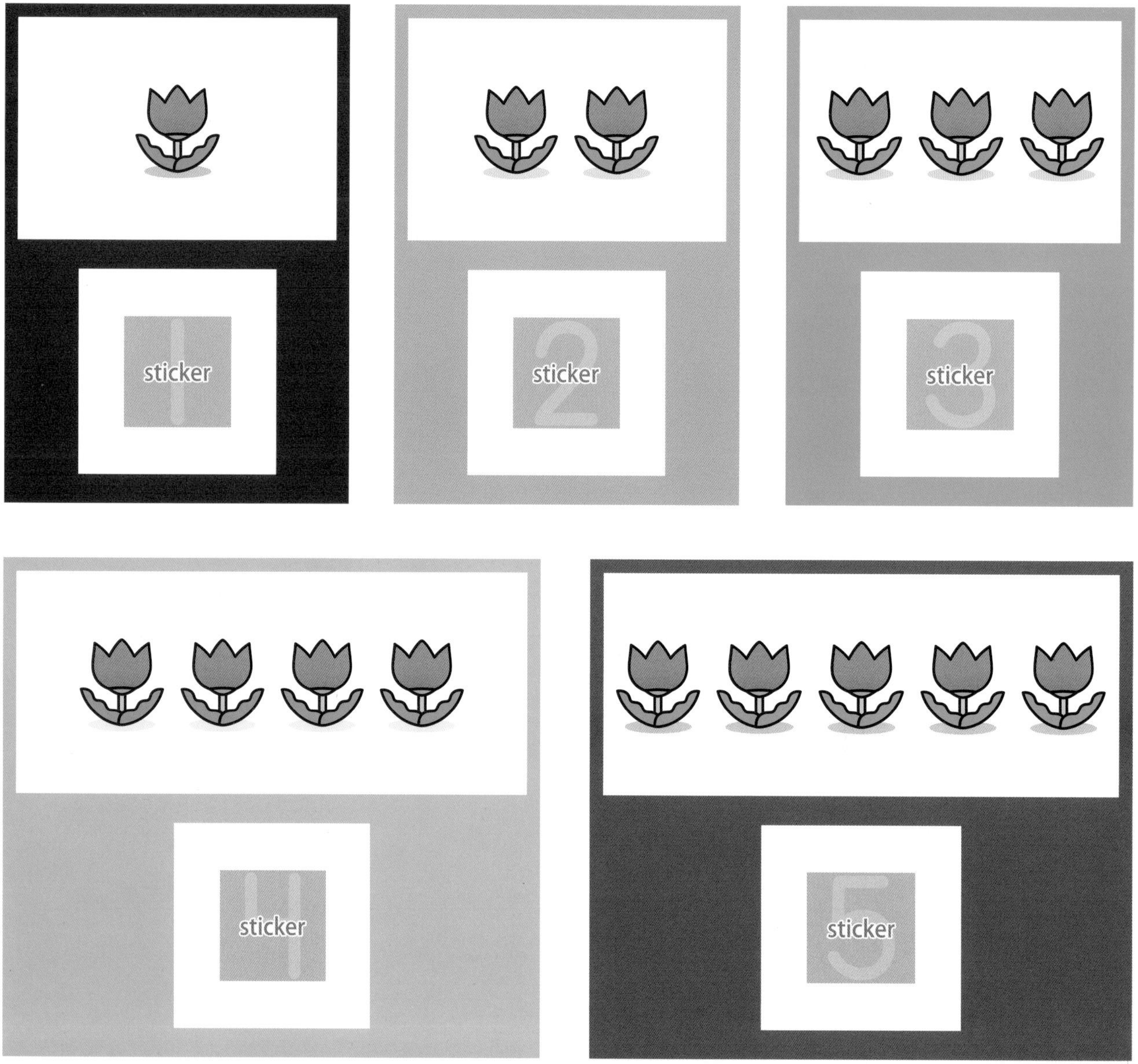

Counting Candy

Count the candy. Add the number sticker to the box that matches the number of candies.

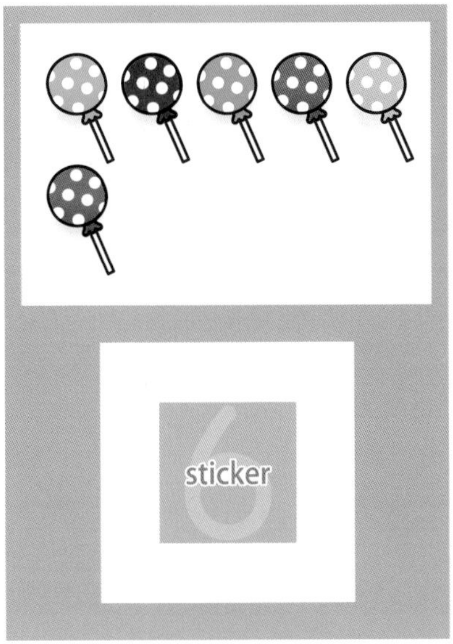

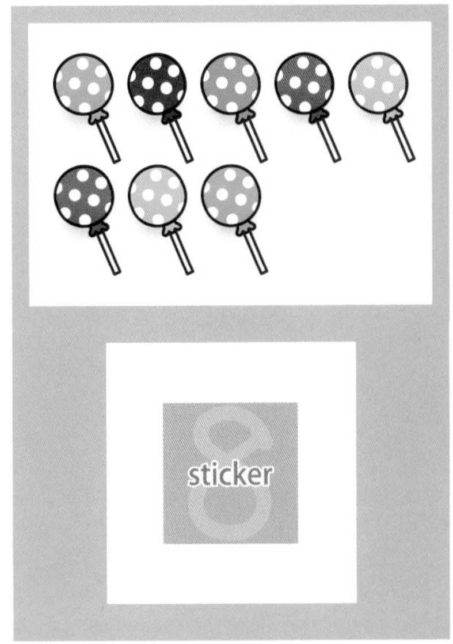

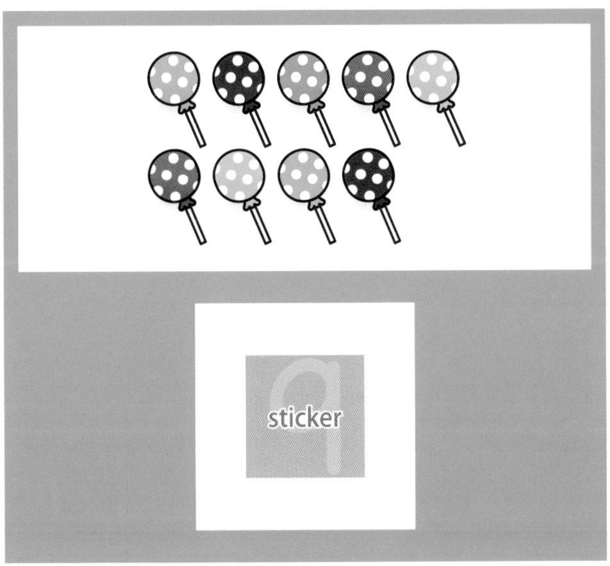

Maze Numbers

Number Maze

Follow the path from ➡ to ➡ in the order of smallest to largest. As you go, put number stickers on the path. When finished, count the number of fish.

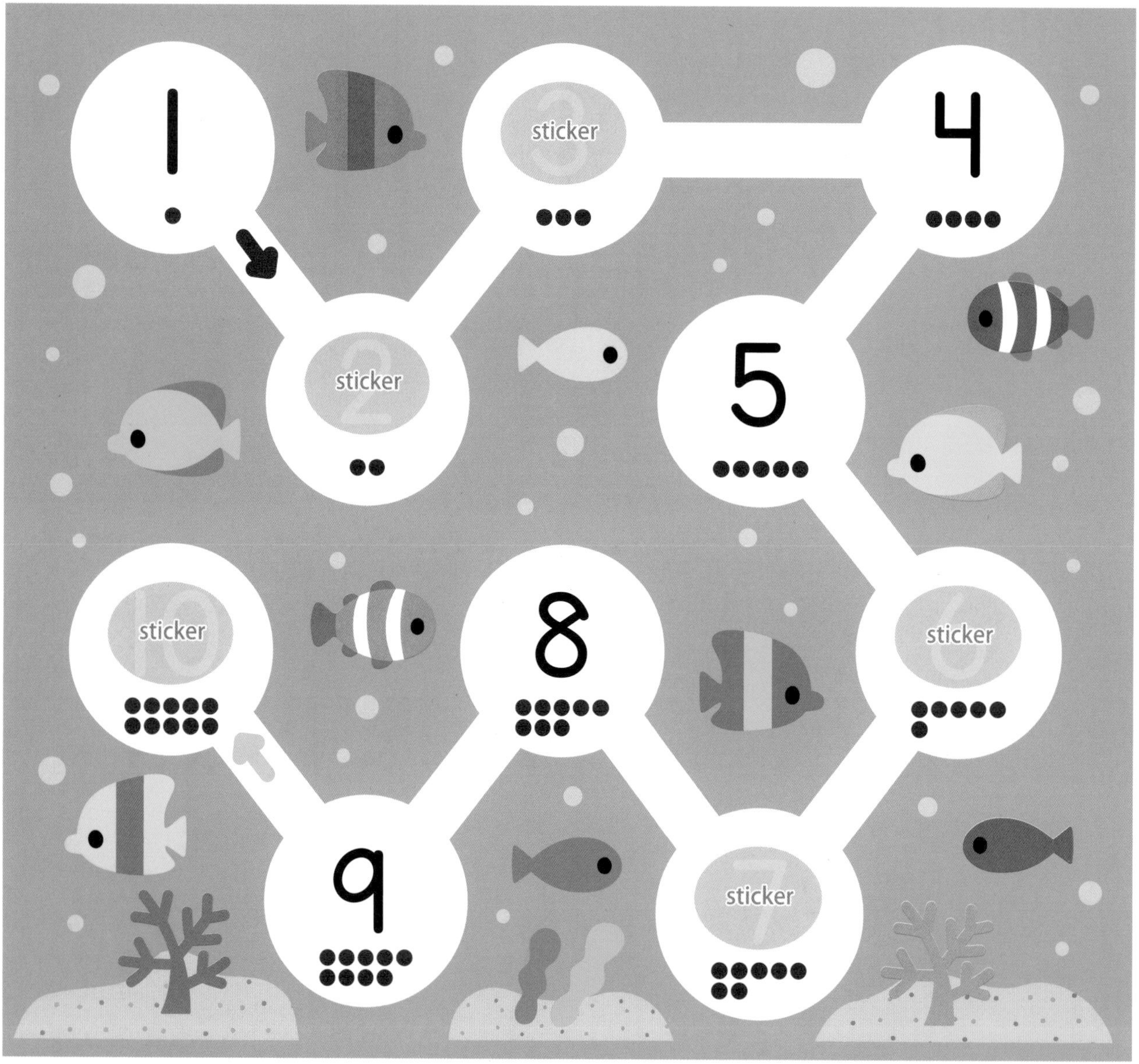

Classification

Things That Go Together

Find the stickers that belong together. Then, put them in each color group.

Sticker
Good job!

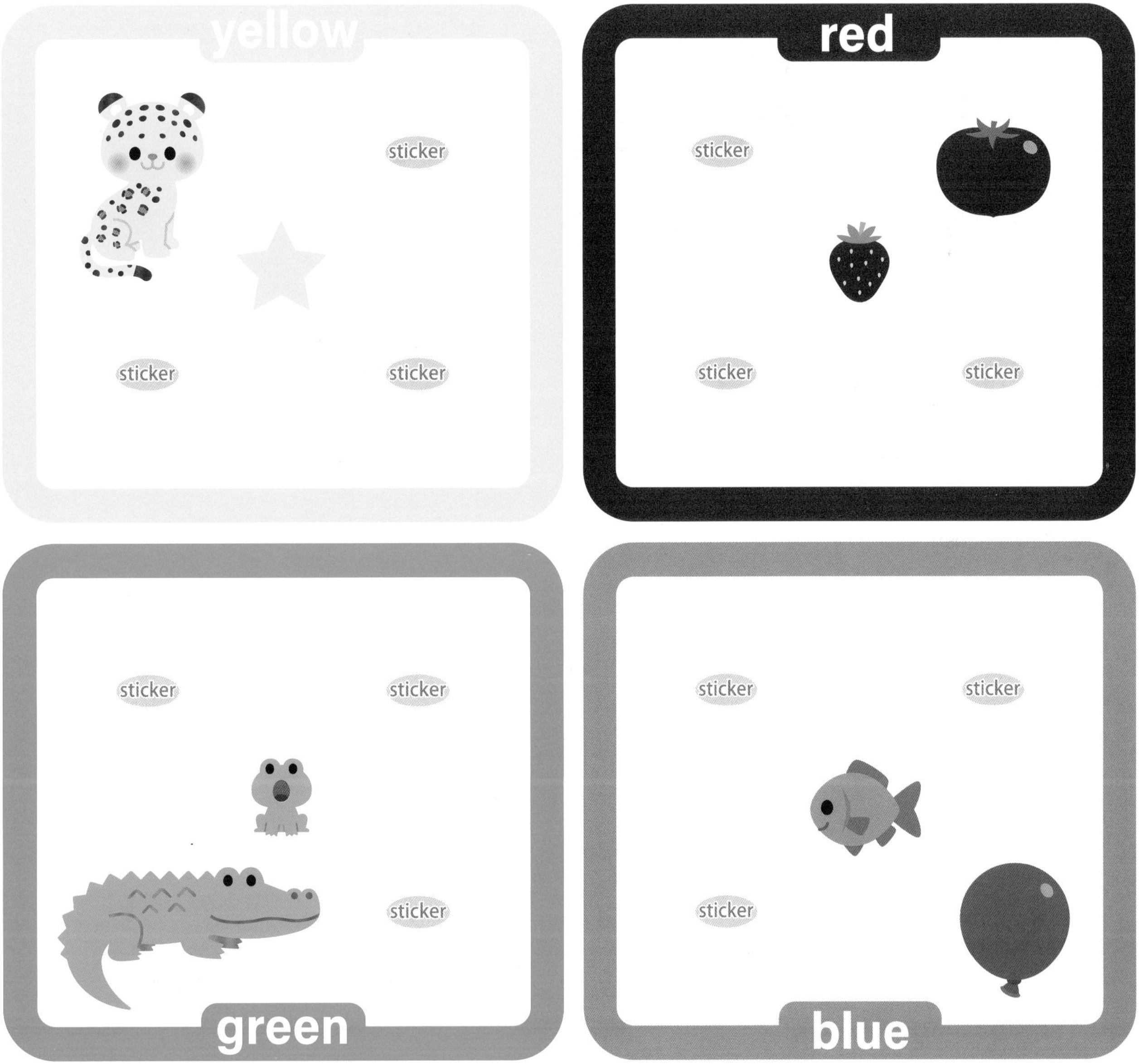

Matching Game

Vehicle Parts

Guess the vehicle from its part. When you name the vehicle, put a sticker on its shadow.

Matching Game

Matching Match

Each picture shows the front of an animal. Put a sticker next to the animal that shows it from the side.

Pattern Play

Follow the path from to while putting stickers on in this order:

Patterns

Pattern Play

Follow the path from ➡ to ➡ while putting stickers on sticker in this order:

Pattern Puzzle

Follow the pattern in the example to create the same pattern in the boxes on the right.

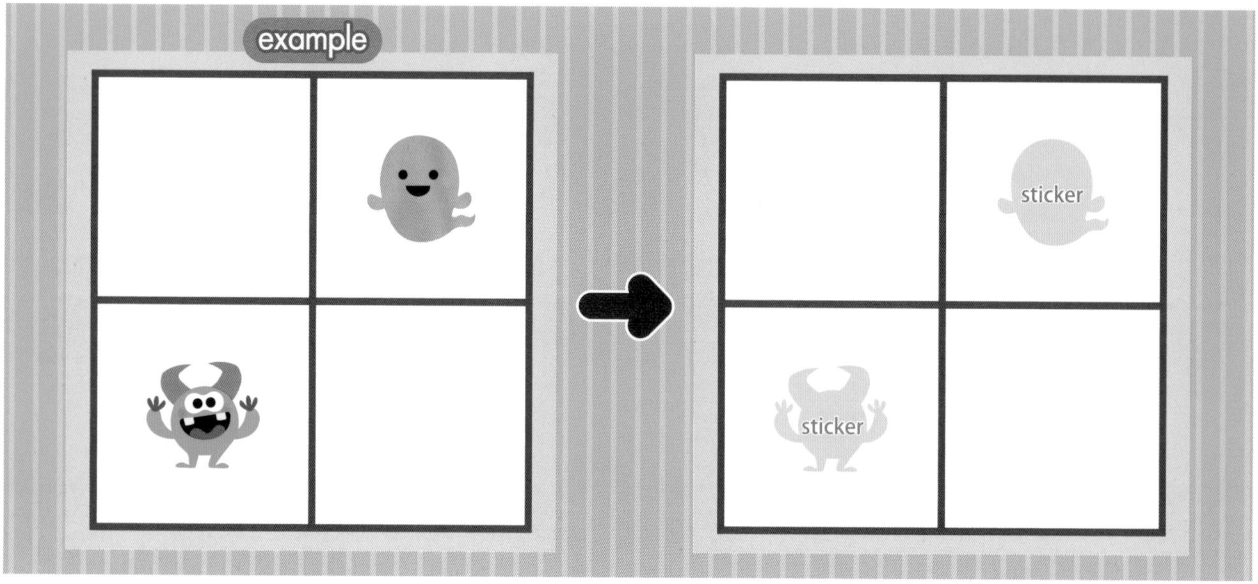

Pattern Puzzle

Follow the pattern in the example to create the same pattern in the boxes on the right.

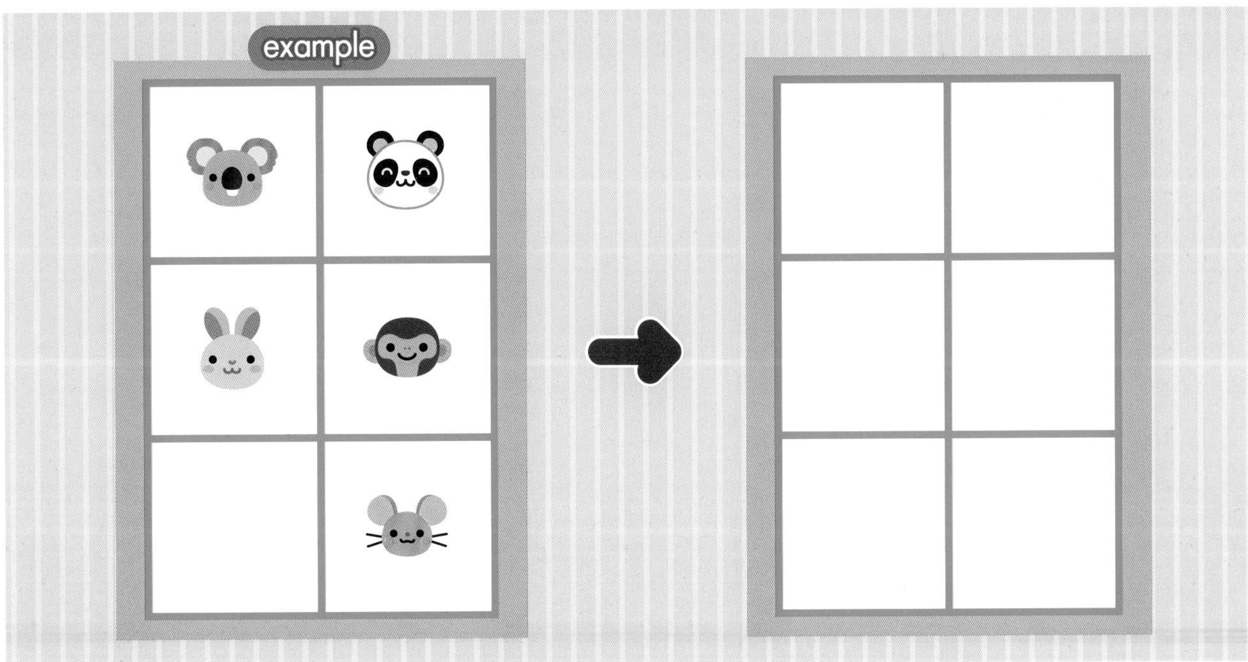

Snack Time

Add stickers so each child's tray has a cheeseburger, a box of french fries, and a cup of juice.

Maze

Fruit Maze

Follow the path from ➡ to ➡ while putting fruit stickers on their matching shadows.

Maze

Connect the Bridges

Connect the missing bridges with stickers. Then, follow the path from ➡ to ➡.

Maze

Fix the Road

Fix the broken road with stickers. Then, follow the path from ➡ to ➡.

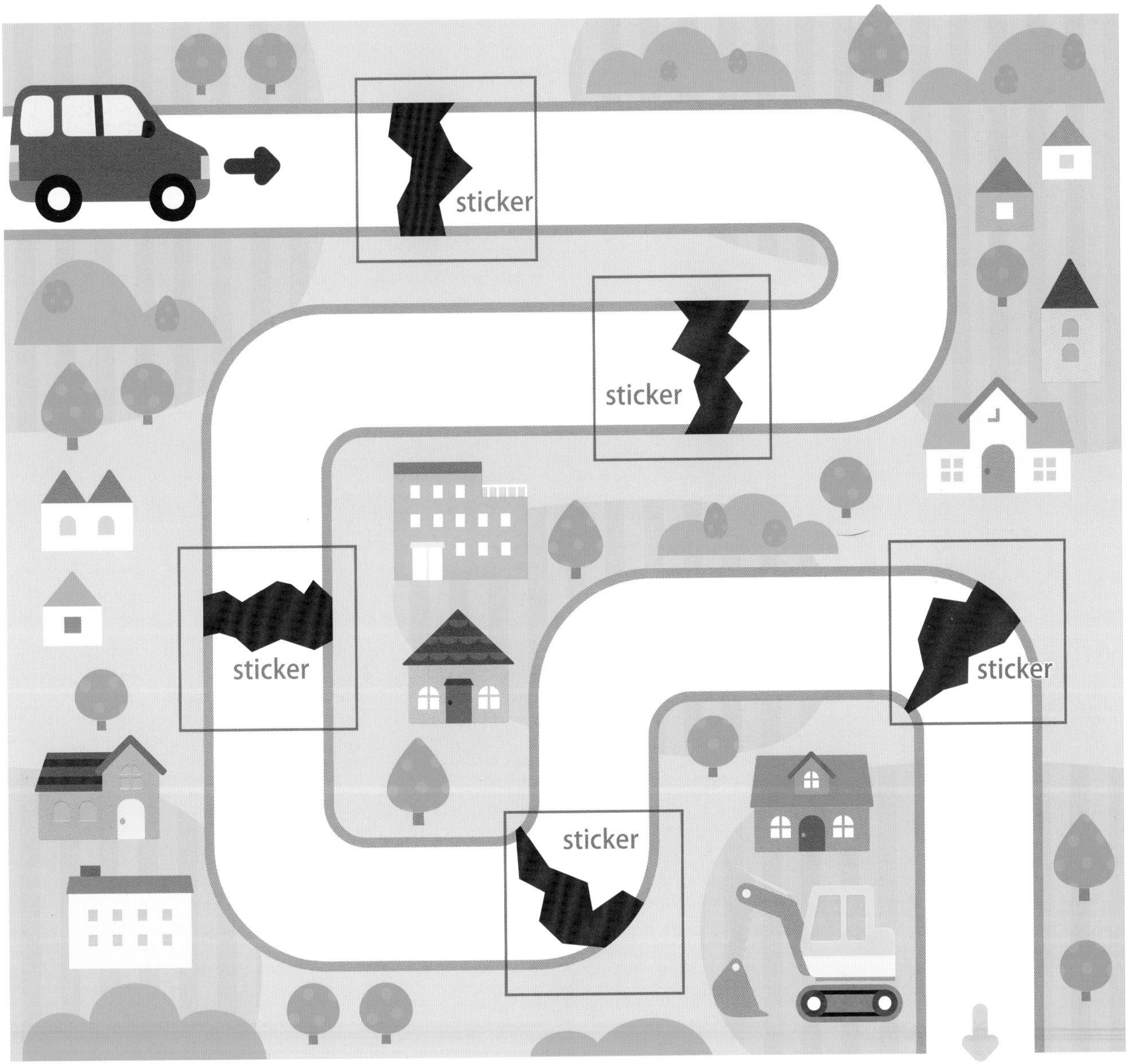

At the Amusement Park

Put ■ ▲ ♥ ★ stickers on their matching shapes to complete the scene.

Creativity

Playground Games

Put playground stickers on the grass wherever you'd like. Then, add animal and flower stickers.

Playroom

Help keep the children's room tidy. Put the book and toy stickers on the correct shelf.

Creativity

Nail Art

Decorate the nails with your favorite stickers.
Then, add the ring stickers.

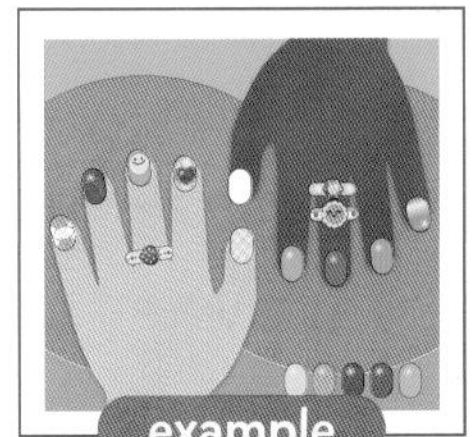

example

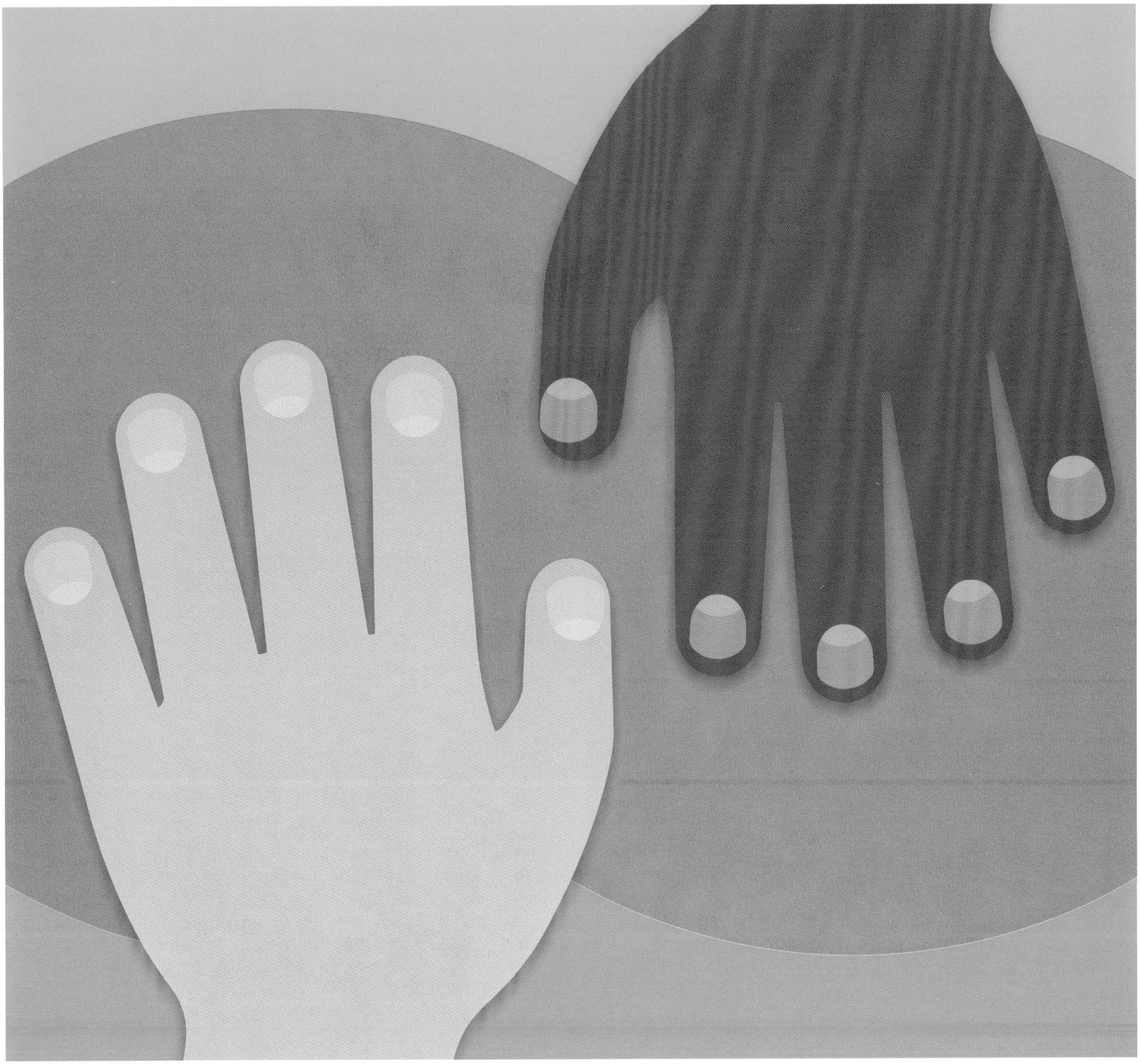

Creativity

Decorate a Bag

Decorate the bag with your favorite stickers.

example

Creativity

Decorate a Dino T-Shirt

Decorate the T-shirt with your favorite stickers.

example

Creativity

Decorate the Outfit

Decorate the dress with stickers.

example

Shapes

Castle Puzzle

Put stickers on the castle so they match the shapes.

Shapes Numbers

Globe Puzzle

Put stickers on the globe so they match the shapes and numbers.

Reward Stickers
Stickers
Good Great Good Good Great Good Good Great Good Good Great Great Great
Great Good Great Great Good Great Great Good Great Great Good Great Good
Good Good Good Good Good Good Good Good Good Good Good Good Good
Great Great Great Great Great Great Great Great Great Great Great Good Great
Page 1
Page 2
Page 3
Page 4

Stickers
Page 5
Page 6
crayon
Page 7
Page 8
Page 9
Page 10
Page 11
Page 12
Page 13

Page 14
Page 15
Page 16
Page 17
Page 18
Page 19
Page 20

Stickers

Page 21

Page 24

Page 22

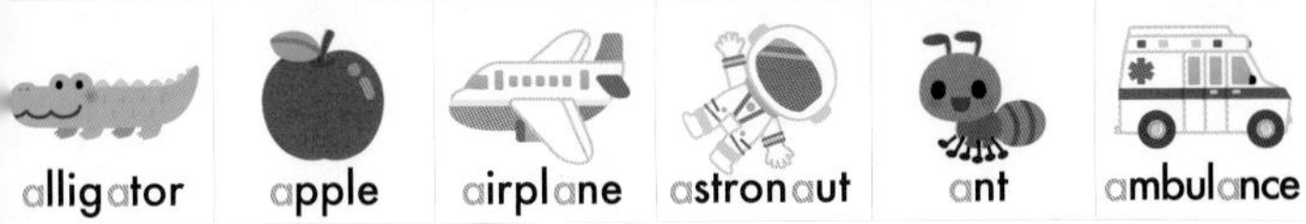

A C F H J

Page 23

1 2 3 4 5
6 7 8 9 10

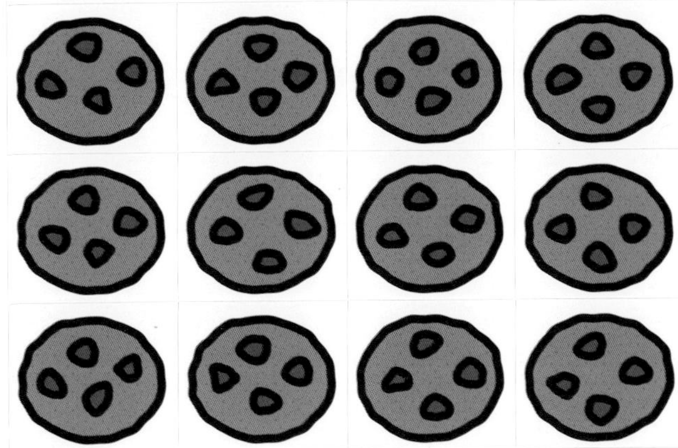

Page 25

Pages 26–27

Page 28

2 3 6 7 10

Page 29

Page 30

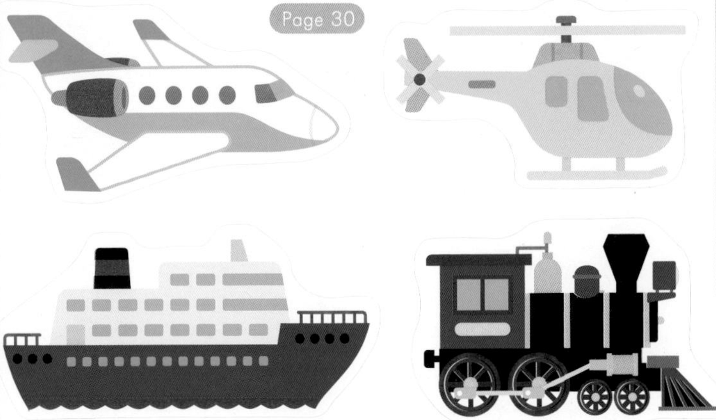

Pages 32–33

Page 31

Pages 34–35

Page 36

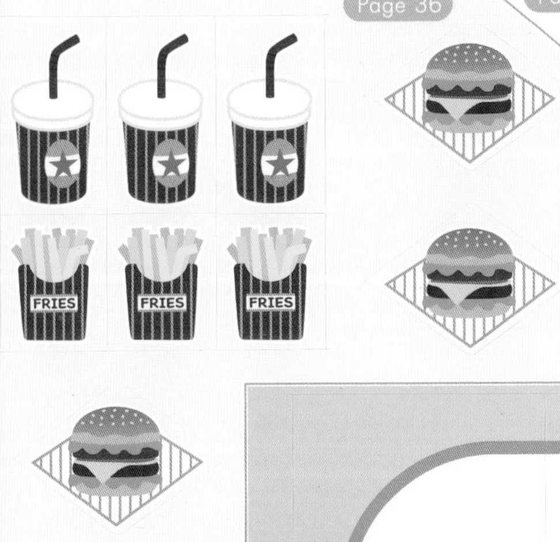

Page 37

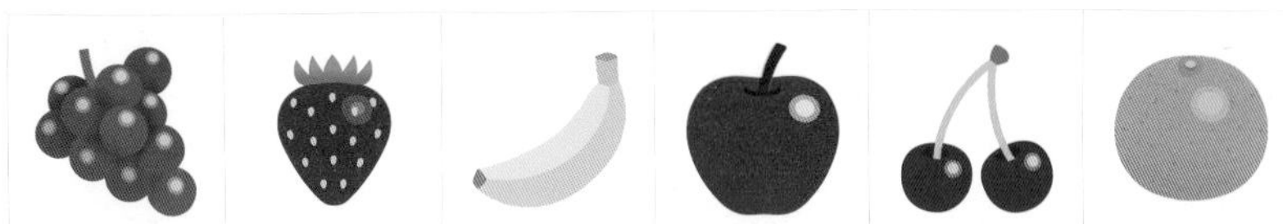

Page 38

Page 39

Page 40
Page 41
Page 42
Page 43
A
B
C